I Am God's Masterpiece

31 Days of Affirmation

Bridgette Marie

I Am God's Masterpiece
31 Days of Affirmation

Copyright © 2018 Bridgette Marie

ESV, English Standard Version
The Holy Bible, English Standard Version. ESV® Text Edition: 2016. Copyright © 2001 by Crossway Bibles, a publishing ministry of Good News Publishers.

GNT, Good News Translation
Copyright © 1992 by American Bible Society

NIV, New International Version
Holy Bible, New International Version®, NIV® Copyright ©1973, 1978, 1984, 2011 by Biblica, Inc.® Used by permission. All rights reserved worldwide.

NLT, New Living Translation
HOLY BIBLE, New Living Translation, copyright © 1996, 2004, 2015 by Tyndale House Foundation. Used by permission of Tyndale House Publishers, Inc., Carol Stream, Illinois 60188. All rights reserved.

Dedication

This book is dedicated to my beautiful mom, Wendy.
Thank you for setting the bar high and teaching me
my worth and how God views me. This has allowed
me to walk in confidence daily, knowing that God
never made a mistake on me. Every single day, I live
my truth because of you.

To my late great grandmothers and great-
grandmothers Lillie Mae "Big Mama," Grandma Josie,
Hazel "Grandmother," Grandma Gaines, and Mama
Bryant. I pull strength from your spirits; you all were
beautiful black queens who taught me so much just
by watching you at my young age. Thank you. I hope
I'm making you all proud.

To my sister Tiffani. Thank you for just being you. We
are so much alike, yet so very different. You've taught
me to be my authentic self no matter who's watching
and to walk in the calling I'm worthy of, never tilting
my crown.

To my oldest sister Nichole and my nieces LaQuisha,
Jordan, Zharia, Makayla, Jade, Kenberly, Monae,
Kaliah, and Ava. I love you all and I want you to see
yourself as God sees you daily, as His masterpiece.
You all give me the push I need daily to keep sharing
God's Word through scripture.

To my aunts, Auntie Nina, Auntie JoAnn, and Auntie
Veronica. Thank you for being light in my life, all my

life. For encouraging and pushing me to be my best. I'm thankful for you.

Thank you, to every woman who has inspired me in some way to write this book. For me, you all have impacted my life in some way: Devyn, Dominique, Daisy, Nikki, Tashana, Todzia, Tonoa, Jayla, Pleshette, Brea, Yolanda, Stephanie, Rorilynn, Azadeh, Aerica, Olga (Godmom), Clarissa, Justyce, Amy, Mama Laura, Auntie Jorine, Barb, Memaw, Auntie Kim, Amber, Ashley, Brandi, Trayonna, Racquel, Dalesha, Jadah, Noe, Enjonette, Mieka, Yoyo, Lasha, Ty'nesha, Lunden, De'Johnnah, Monique, Brittney, Candice, Melody, Shaquida, Janaii, Minster Rita, Pastor Carol, Jasemyn, Sherill, Nadine, Sister Sylvia, Keisha, Briana, Shaufon, Melanie, Brooke, India, Morgan, Mrs. Westbrooks, Andreia, Jade, Jackie, Kim, Veronica, Adriana, and Lynn.

To the ladies in my Connection Group, thank you. Sitting with me weekly helps me give you all that God has given me, which in turn strengthens me for this journey God has me on. We are connected for life.

Lastly, I dedicate this book to my unborn son Josiah. You have really helped me dig deep into my soul to put this book together. It is my prayer that your dad and I will teach you how to treat a woman and how God views women so that you are the gentleman we will raise you to be. I hope to give one of these books to your future wife and daughters. I love you, son. You gave me the push I needed to complete this book.

Contents

Day 1: I am completely accepted

Titus 3:7 (ESV)

So that being justified by his grace we might become heirs according to the hope of eternal life.

"The world doesn't have to accept me; my creator completely accepts me."

You are completely accepted by God! There is nothing that you can say or do that will allow God to turn away from you or revoke your privilege of being His child. The amazing thing about God is that He does not treat us as this world treats us, nor as our sins deserve. We don't have to have the latest fashion, the biggest house, the most expensive car, the best hair, the flawless makeup, the most money, be a particular size, or hang around the most popular people to be accepted by Him. He loves and accepts us just the way we are.

At this point in your life, have you completely accepted who God created you to be?

Look deep within yourself. See the person that God created—not the person who is wearing a mask, not the person who is trying to be who they see on television and not the person who isn't living in her truth. See the person who has flaws, the person who is not perfect, the person who is living with her truth, the person who accepts that she is a work in progress. This is the person God loves and completely accepts. It is time for you to fully accept her!

Don't allow the world's views to dictate how you view yourself. If you can see yourself from God's perspective, you'll understand why He completely accepts you, which He created unselfishly. You are a great design handcrafted by the Master's hands. God never made a mistake on you. Despite how you feel about yourself, you need to recognize that God completely accepts you. The fact that God has completely accepted you, should give way to you completely accepting who He created you to be.

I am God's masterpiece, and I have been completely accepted.

- Genesis 4:7 (ESV)
- Ephesians 1:5-6 (NLT)
- Psalm 27:10 (GNT)

Prayer for Today

Thank you, Lord, for completely accepting me and for making me a great creation for your kingdom. Help me to love and accept every flaw that I have and use it for your glory. I want to see myself from your perspective so that I can fully accept who you created me to be. Help me to remove the mask that I so often hide behind. I know who I am in you and I want to fully walk in who you have called me to be on this earth. In Jesus' name, amen.

Notes

_____

_____

_____

_____

_____

_____

_____

_____

_____

_____

_____

_____

_____

_____

_____

Day 2: I am loved unconditionally

Isaiah 54:10 (GNT)

The mountains and hills may crumble, but my love for you will never end; I will keep forever my promise of peace. So says the Lord who loves you.

"I am a product of God, and He loves me unconditionally."

There is no greater love than the love from God. We know certain people in our lives who love us, but there is no one who loves us unconditionally like God loves us. He proves to us daily how much He truly loves us by providing for us, going before us, protecting us, making sure we are well taken care of, never turning His back on us, and showing us how to love ourselves as well as others. God's love will never fail because He is the definition of love.

Do you realize that God's love will never fail you because He loves you unconditionally?

Unconditional love has no limitations, no restrictions, no boundaries, and no conditions. There is no limit to how much God will love you. There is no restriction on the way God shows love toward you. There is no boundary that God sets to how much He loves you. There is no condition that will make God stop loving you. The limits, restrictions, boundaries, and conditions that the world sets on love do not meet the standards of unconditional love that God has for His children.

As we understand the meaning behind the unconditional love that God shows us daily, we will begin to love ourselves as God loves us. We will begin to see ourselves as a beautiful creation handcrafted by God. The love of God goes beyond your physical appearance. God loves everything about you, mind, body, and spirit.

You will never meet a person in this lifetime who has an unconditional love for you like God does.

I am God's masterpiece, and He loves me unconditionally.

- Psalm 52:8 (NLT)
- Ephesians 3:17-19 (GNT)
- Romans 8:35 (ESV)
- Psalm 136:2 (NIV)

Prayer for Today

Thank you for loving me unconditionally God. I am so grateful for your unconditional love. Please show me how to love myself as you love me. Thank you for never turning your back on me when I needed your love the most. Thank you for continuing to love me despite the fact that I fail you daily. Give me a pure heart to love others and myself like you love. You are the greatest example of what love is, help me to exhibit the love that you show me daily. In Jesus' name, amen.

Notes

_____

_____

_____

_____

_____

_____

_____

_____

_____

_____

_____

_____

_____

_____

_____

_____

Day 3: I am totally forgiven

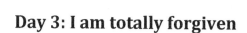

Romans 8:1 (ESV)

There is therefore now no condemnation for those who are in Christ Jesus.

"I am totally forgiven; therefore, I am totally free."

We serve a forgiving God who doesn't treat us how our sins deserve. We've done a lot of negative things in our lives, some things that we may not be too proud of, things that haven't hit light yet, things that we have buried deep, things that we may be embarrassed about, or things that are just down right not of God. All of those things can be forgiven. God is nothing like men, and He holds nothing against you.

God will totally forgive you; have you totally forgiven yourself?

It's time to totally forgive yourself for all that has taken place in your life that you are blaming yourself for. God doesn't blame you. In fact, He wants that burden lifted from you today. Forgiveness equals freedom. In order to walk in what God has in store for you, you must forgive yourself and others. The burden of unforgiveness is too heavy for you to bear. Let it go!

Totally forgiven means that you are totally free. Free from guilt. Free from shame. Free from your past. Free from what others say about you. Free from the negative thoughts that you say about yourself. Free to be who God created you to be.

Free to live out your purpose in the present, despite your past.

Don't allow your past to hinder what God is doing in your present and what He will do in your future. When you go before God, forgive others and He will forgive you. God loves you so much that He doesn't treat you like your sins deserve.

I am God's masterpiece, and I am totally forgiven.

- Mark 11:25 (NLT)
- Psalm 103:12 (GNT)
- Daniel 9:9 (NIV)
- Hebrews 10:17 (ESV)
- Ephesians 1:7 (NLT)
- Acts 3:19 (ESV)

Prayer for Today

Thank you, God, for totally forgiving me. Thank you, God, for setting me free from my past mistakes. When I go forth, I will go forth in power knowing that you don't treat me as my sins deserve. I don't always make the right decisions in life, but you never hold that against me. Teach me to forgive others totally and wholeheartedly. Help me to forgive others and myself as you forgive me. In Jesus' name, amen.

Notes

_____

_____

_____

_____

_____

_____

_____

_____

_____

_____

_____

_____

_____

_____

_____

_____

Day 4: I am extremely valuable

1 Corinthians 7:23 (NLT)

God paid a high price for you, so don't be enslaved by the world.

"I have a purpose in this world, and I am an asset to God's kingdom."

When you know your worth, you won't ever settle for less than you deserve. You are extremely valuable to God and to His kingdom. There is no one in this world who is exactly like you. That means that you bring something unique to the table, a piece of the puzzle that no other person can fit into. God has set you apart, and there is no monetary value that can amount to how valuable you are to God.

Do you realize how extremely valuable you are to God and His kingdom?

God wouldn't have created you if He didn't think you were valuable to His kingdom. You are somebody in this world, you have purpose, you are an asset to the kingdom of God, you will reach individuals for the kingdom of God, you are anointed, you have been called, you have been chosen, and there is no limit to what God plans to do through you.

Your life has been bought with the blood of Jesus. That alone should tell you that you are invaluable. What you wear, what you drive, what you live in, and how much you make do not determine your worth. God already stamped you with value the day that Jesus Christ died on the cross for your sins.

Recognize your worth and never settle for less than God is willing to give you.

I am God's masterpiece, and I am extremely valuable.

- Jeremiah 29:11 (ESV)
- 1 Peter 1:18-19 (NIV)
- 2 Corinthians 5:17 (GNT)
- Ephesians 2:4-7 (NLT)

Prayer for Today

Thank you, God, for making me a valuable asset to your kingdom. Help me to recognize my worth through Jesus Christ. Allow me to never settle for less than I deserve in this lifetime. Thank you for choosing me and for setting me apart. Help me to never be materialistic, as I know that my value is not determined by what I have. Keep my focus on you as I totally surrender to your guidance and help me be an example for others to follow. In Jesus' name, amen.

Notes

_____

_____

_____

_____

_____

_____

_____

_____

_____

_____

_____

_____

_____

_____

_____

Day 5: I am fearfully and wonderfully made

Psalm 139:14 (NLT)

Thank you for making me so wonderfully complex! Your workmanship is marvelous—how well I know it.

"I am an imperfect person, made by a perfect God."

Each day of your life should be a day that you are thanking God that He took time out to create you. Not only did God think of you before He created you, He created you with a purpose and unique design. God created you in His image; you are an imperfect person made by a perfect God.

When you look at yourself in the mirror, what do you see?

From today forward, see a masterpiece of God's handiwork when you look at yourself in the mirror. From the crown of your head to the soles of your feet, God created you in His image and likeness. Everything you see when looking in the mirror, God said is good and perfect in His sight. Don't allow the judgment of the world to cancel out what God perfectly created—which is you.

It's time to accept your flaws and to see yourself as God sees you, His perfect creation. He didn't make you in His image and likeness so that you would hate it or want to change it. He gave you your body type, your features, your hair, your skin tone, your eyes, and your stature because that is what He wanted for you. Once you accept everything about yourself and love yourself like God loves you, you will begin to live in freedom like God wants you to.

I Am God's Masterpiece

Stop self-shaming and/or allowing others to shame you because you don't look like what others think you should look like. Bask in the fact that God made you a beautiful creation.

I am fearfully and wonderfully made, and I am God's masterpiece.

- Psalm 92:4-5 (NLT)
- Psalm 104:24 (ESV)
- Genesis 1:27 (NIV)

Prayer for Today

Thank you, God, for making me a beautiful creation. Help me to accept myself as you accept me and to love myself like you love me. I am thankful that you created me in your image and likeness. Help me to see beauty when I look at myself in the mirror. I don't want to shame myself because I don't look like the next person. I no longer want to compare myself to others, because I know you created me perfectly like you wanted me to be. Work on me Lord from the inside out. In Jesus' name, amen.

Notes

_____

_____

_____

_____

_____

_____

_____

_____

_____

_____

_____

_____

_____

_____

_____

_____

Day 6: I am chosen by God

John 15:16 (NLT)

You didn't choose me. I chose you. I appointed you to go and produce lasting fruit, so that the Father will give you whatever you ask for, using my name.

"I am more than what the eye can see, God chose me."

It's amazing to realize that God chose you before your creation. You had a purpose even before you were born. God placed you in His royal priesthood, He set you apart and He has given you an assignment while on this earth. There is nothing that you will face on this earth that God didn't choose for you. Even when you don't make the best decisions in life, God chose this life for you.

Are you willing to do exactly what God chose for you to do on this earth?

In order to fulfill your purpose here on earth, you must begin by asking God to reveal your purpose to you. Then, you must begin to fully walk in it. There is a chosen road that God has specifically for you. The only way that you will know your path is by spending an ample amount of time with Him. No one but God can tell you what your purpose here on earth is. No one else in this world chose you for this life but God alone.

Never underestimate what God can do through you and where He is taking you. To be one of the chosen ones, there is much required of you. There are so many people watching you and counting on you. Not everyone would be fit for this life; that's why God gave it to you. He knew whom you'd reach, who'd listen to you, and whom you'd lead to His kingdom for His glory.

Your life was created with purpose. God chose you for the things that you will see and endure in this lifetime. Nothing put on you will be too hard for you to bear. You were born for this life and God chose you because He knew you would be perfect for the assignment at hand.

God has chosen me, and I am God's masterpiece.

- 1 Peter 2:9 (NIV)
- Deuteronomy 7:6 (ESV)
- Ephesians 2:10 (GNT)

Prayer for Today

Thank you, God, for choosing me. This life gets tough for me sometimes, but I know you chose me for it. Help me to see my life from your perspective. I want to live according to your will. Thank you for the assignments that you have given me, and the people that I will reach for your kingdom. Reveal my purpose to me so that I can fully walk in it. I'm thankful that you chose me to be a part of your royal priesthood. I don't take being a chosen daughter of the King lightly. In Jesus' name, amen.

Notes

_____

_____

_____

_____

_____

_____

_____

_____

_____

_____

_____

_____

_____

_____

Day 7: I am powerful beyond measure

2 Corinthians 12:10 (NLT)

That's why I take pleasure in my weaknesses, and in the insults, hardships, persecutions, and troubles that I suffer for Christ. For when I am weak, then I am strong.

"Even in my weakness,
I am made strong."

God has given you the power that you need to overcome every obstacle that you will ever face on this earth. The more time you spend with God, the more powerful you will become. Even in your weakness, God will give you strength so that your weakness can turn into strength. You are powerful beyond measure. Begin to walk in the power that God has given you.

Do you recognize the power that God has given you?

The power that you possess is a power that can only come from the true living God. Nothing or no one that you will ever encounter in this life is more powerful than God alone. The amazing thing about God is that He gives you power over the enemy of your soul; yes, you have power over Satan. Power to make him flee, power to stand strong even when he's throwing darts at you, strength not to give in, strength not to give up, strength to overcome, strength to endure, and strength to keep going despite what situations and circumstances you face.

There is no measure to the power that God has given you. When you understand the strength that you have through Jesus Christ, you'll understand why God turned your weaknesses into strengths.

Learn to walk in the power that you possess through Jesus and be willing to follow the commands from God daily.

I am powerful beyond measure, and I am God's masterpiece.

- Philippians 4:13 (GNT)
- Isaiah 40:31 (ESV)
- 2 Timothy 1:7 (NIV)
- Luke 10:19 (ESV)
- 1 Corinthians 4:20 (GNT)

Prayer for Today

Thank you, God, for your power over the enemy. Power to crush strongholds. Power to make Satan flee. Power to plead the blood of Jesus. I know that through your power I can do anything that you give me the power to fulfill. Thank you, Lord, for turning my weaknesses into strengths. Help me to recognize that you are continually working on me. Whatever you have me to do from this point forward, I shall do through your strength and power. In Jesus' name, amen.

Notes

_____

_____

_____

_____

_____

_____

_____

_____

_____

_____

_____

_____

_____

_____

_____

Day 8: I am respected

Matthew 7:12 (NIV)

So in everything, do to others what you would have them do to you, for this sums up the Law and the Prophets.

"When I step on the scene, the Holy spirit shifts the atmosphere."

We are taught that in order to receive respect, one must give respect. Whether you believe this to be true or not, you should demand respect wherever you go. It doesn't have to be verbal. As a child of God, you should have a posture that you are heir to the throne of God, because you are. This doesn't mean you should be cocky or arrogant, but you are daughter to the King of Kings.

Can you feel the shift when you step on the scene?

You may not realize the role you play in the kingdom, but your role is important. We should respect everyone who has a role in the kingdom of God. Don't look down on others; they play a vital role just like you do. So, the next time you go to roll your eyes, turn your nose up, or gossip about the next person, remember that they are a vital part to God's kingdom.

There are so many people in this life who look up to you and respect you. Don't let those individuals down by disrespecting yourself or others. If you haven't figured out what purpose you have in this world, allow God to reveal it to you daily. This will allow you to see that every child of God is a part of the same royal priesthood that you belong to. Learn to check yourself. As you demand respect, give respect as much as you want to receive it.

I am respected, and I am God's masterpiece.

- Titus 2:7-8 (NLT)
- Romans 13:2 (ESV)
- Luke 14:10 (NIV)

Prayer for Today

Lord, purge me right now of everything that is not like you. Help me to see others and myself from your perspective. I know that when I step on the scene, the Holy Spirit shifts the atmosphere on my behalf. You have created me heir to your throne and I thank you. Thank you for thinking enough of me to bring me out of darkness into the marvelous light. Help me to respect others and myself and to be a great example for those who are watching me. In Jesus' name, amen.

Notes

_____

_____

_____

_____

_____

_____

_____

_____

_____

_____

_____

_____

_____

_____

_____

_____

I Am God's Masterpiece

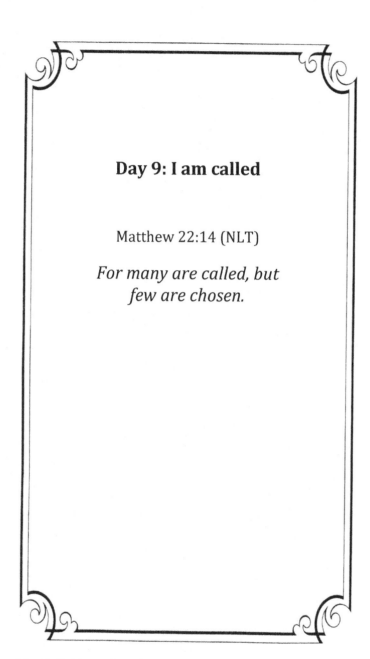

Day 9: I am called

Matthew 22:14 (NLT)

For many are called, but few are chosen.

"Nothing in this world could ever amount to the calling on my life."

God has turned you from the victim into the victor. Nothing that has happened to you is because of luck or chance; it all has to do with the calling on your life. Whether you realize it right now or not, everything in this life that Satan meant for evil, God turned around for your good. You were born for this life; God chose you for it.

Have you answered the calling on your life?

Now that you know that you've been called to this life, it's time to walk in your calling. It's never too late for God to reveal your purpose to you and it's never too late for you to walk in it. There is a reason that you were born and before you die, you will have fulfilled the calling that God has on your life. Don't be ashamed of what you've been through; your testimony is powerful.

You have what it takes to be exactly what God has called you to be on the earth. You don't need to change anything about yourself. Allow God to strip you of anything that is not like Him and add to you all that He has entitled you to. Don't put off your calling because you are afraid of what all it includes. If you trust God, you know that He has the master plan and it will never fail.

Your main goal when walking in the calling that God has for you is to live an authentic life that is pleasing to God. You will lead others to Jesus through your walk.

I have been called, and I am God's masterpiece.

- Philippians 1:6 (NIV)
- Luke 12:32 (ESV)
- Romans 8:28 (ESV)
- 1 Corinthians 1:26 (NIV)

Prayer for Today

Thank you, Lord, for the calling on my life. I don't know what all it entails, but I do trust you Lord. Help me to walk with purpose in my calling. I don't want to be afraid of the unknown. Help me to have faith in you like never before. I know there are individuals out there for me to reach for your kingdom. Help me to identify the individuals who you have assigned to me and help me be a great example to them. In Jesus' name, amen.

Notes

_____

_____

_____

_____

_____

_____

_____

_____

_____

_____

_____

_____

_____

_____

_____

_____

_____

Day 10: I am anointed

2 Corinthians 1:21-22 (ESV)

And it is God who establishes us with you in Christ, and has anointed us, and who has also put his seal on us and given us his Spirit in our hearts as a guarantee.

"There is nothing that you can do to me that God won't allow; I am His anointed one."

There is nothing that anyone can do to remove the anointing from you. When God gives, He's the only one who can take away. You may have never felt God's anointing on you, but that doesn't mean that it doesn't exist. You have been anointed to live this life that God has ordained for you and to touch the individuals who God has assigned to you.

Are you walking in the anointing that God has for your life?

Be very clear when it comes to anointing. When God established us with Jesus, He put a seal on us and anointed us while giving us His spirit in our hearts. You do have an anointing over your life. An anointing that the world didn't give you and the world can't take away.

As God's anointed, He will protect you at all costs. There is nothing that God won't do for you. He commands that those who are out to get you will be rebuked, those who want to do you harm will not, and every trap set up by the enemy for you will fail. Understand your position and the anointment that is over your life, given to you by God. All you need to do now is walk in it!

God anoints me, and I am God's masterpiece!

- Psalm 45:7 (NLT)
- 1 Chronicles 16:21-22 (GNT)

Prayer for Today

Lord, thank you for the anointing that is over my life. Help me to feel your anointing and walk in boldness knowing that you have given me your anointing over my life. I may not always be aware of it, but I believe your Word, and I know it is true. Help me to walk in your anointing all the days of my life as I honor you. Not only do I ask that I feel your anointing daily, but allow others whom I come in contact with to feel your anointing through me. Thank you for your anointing and for choosing me. In Jesus' name, amen.

Notes

_____

_____

_____

_____

_____

_____

_____

_____

_____

_____

_____

_____

_____

_____

Day 11: I am to die for

John 3:16 (ESV)

For God so loved the world, that he gave His only Son, that whoever believes in him should not perish but have eternal life.

"You're literally to die for;
Jesus Christ died for you."

Take it all in when remembering that Jesus Christ actually did die FOR YOU! You were on Jesus' mind when He was nailed to the cross. He thought so much of you that He endured all that pain and suffering so that you would be able to live freely without so much pain and suffering.

Never underestimate how much you actually mean to God. There is nothing or no one who can compare to God and the sacrifice of His only son on the cross. It means that He thought the world of you, and that you're unique and special to Him.

How can you express your joy today by letting Jesus know you are appreciative of Him dying on the cross for you?

No matter what you face on a daily basis, remember that you're special to God. Never underestimate how much God thinks of you on a daily basis. Whenever you feel alone, sad, mad, or confused, remember the person who carried your burdens on His back when He carried the cross and was crucified on your behalf. You matter so much that you are literally to die for.

Be determined to live your best life knowing that Jesus Christ sacrificed His life in order to bring you new life. You are truly something special.

I am to die for, and I am God's masterpiece.

- John 10:28 (NIV)
- 1 Peter 3:18 (ESV)
- John 15:13 (GNT)
- Romans 5:8 (NLT)

Prayer for Today

Thank you, God, for sending your son to die for me on the cross. Help me to feel a sense of satisfaction knowing that you had me on your mind even before I stepped foot on the earth. Don't ever let me take for granted what you did for me. Help me to live each day to its full potential knowing that you sacrificed your son so that I could live a life that is pleasing to you. I'm forever grateful for your sacrifice, Lord. I thank you for always keeping me in mind. In Jesus' name, amen.

Notes

_____

_____

_____

_____

_____

_____

_____

_____

_____

_____

_____

_____

_____

_____

_____

_____

I Am God's Masterpiece

Day 12: I am qualified

Ephesians 2:10 (ESV)

For we are His workmanship, created in Christ Jesus for good works, which God prepared beforehand, that we should walk in them.

"I don't need the world's approval;
I am qualified by God's standards."

We oftentimes view ourselves from the world's
eyes instead of God's eyes. We tear ourselves down
by thinking that we should come close to what we
see on television or in magazines. But God qualified
you to be who you are supposed to be in this life
based on who He created you to be. We oftentimes
disqualify ourselves because we think others are
more qualified than we are.

As God's masterpiece, He has qualified you to be
the head and not the tail, to be above and not
beneath, to be the lender and not the borrower. You
have to believe that you are qualified to be great.
You may not have all the glitz and glamour right
now, but you have all the tools inside of you that
God gave you to complete your job on earth.

God has qualified you for greatness and He will
place the right resources, people, and places in your
life so that you can fulfill your purpose. Don't doubt
what God can do for you and through you. When
you surrender all to God, you'll see how qualified
you truly are through Him. He will show you things
that only the qualified, anointed, and chosen
witness in this lifetime: miracles and blessings.

Remember never to disqualify yourself because God qualified you. You are an important person to God and your very being makes God smile.

I am qualified, and I am God's masterpiece.

- Isaiah 6:8 (GNT)
- Jeremiah 29:11 (NIV)
- Philippians 2:13 (NLT)

Prayer for Today

Lord, thank you for qualifying me to be who you called me to be on this earth. Help me not to feel less than, discouraged, or disqualified by anyone on this earth. I don't know all that you've called me to do or be on this earth, but I am ready for the greatness that you have qualified me for. Help me reach nations for your kingdom. Help me to have the right attitude knowing that I'm qualified to do what you've called me to do, to be who you called me to be, and to reach who you called me to reach. In Jesus' name, amen.

Notes

_____

_____

_____

_____

_____

_____

_____

_____

_____

_____

_____

_____

_____

_____

_____

Day 13: I am not my past

Philippians 3:13 (NIV)

Brothers and sisters, I do not consider myself yet to have taken hold of it. But one thing I do: Forgetting what is behind and straining toward what is ahead.

"That's my past,
I don't live there anymore."

You are not your past. You don't have to live in the past, nor do you have to allow others to hold your past against you. You may have failed, you may have done some things that you aren't proud of, and people may have written you off. Good thing, you're not your past. Every day is a new day to make a change.

Don't allow your past to have power over you. It should not hinder your growth, it should not stop you from committing to things that benefit you, it should not hold you back from greatness, and it should not make you feel like you should be punished for the rest of your life. You are not your past.

Can you confidently put your past behind you?

God wants you to walk in boldness knowing that, in Him, you have been made a new creature and who you are now is not who you used to be. Be thankful that God does not hold your past against you and that He can use the person you are right now to fulfill your divine purpose on this earth.

The longer you allow your past to hinder your growth, the longer it will take to get to the beautiful destiny that God has aligned for your life.

Remember, your past is behind you, so refuse to go backwards.

I am not my past; I am God's masterpiece.

- Isaiah 43:18 (NLT)
- Proverbs 24:16 (NIV)
- Philippians 3:12 (ESV)
- Psalm 37:23-26 (NLT)
- Psalm 54:4 (GNT)

Prayer for Today

Lord, thank you for renewing me daily. I know that I am not my past, so don't allow my past to hinder me in the calling that you have on my life. You want to do great things with my life and I accept all that you have for me. Instill in me that my future will be bright because you have total control over it. The tests I have endured have been added to my testimony and that is the only time I will revisit my past. Thank you for helping me recover from my past and for not holding it against me. Make my future all that you want it to be. In Jesus' name, amen.

Notes

_____

_____

_____

_____

_____

_____

_____

_____

_____

_____

_____

_____

_____

_____

_____

_____

I Am God's Masterpiece

Day 14: I am whole

Colossians 2:10 (ESV)

*And you have been filled in him,
who is the head of all rule
and authority.*

"I am made whole through Jesus Christ. I am nothing without Him."

If ever you are feeling incomplete in this life, you haven't been spending enough time with your creator (God). There is no person or thing that can make you whole on this earth. You don't have to have the finest things in life to be or feel whole. Your mate does not make you whole. Being popular or famous does not make you whole. If all those things were stripped from you, you would still be whole through Christ Jesus, our Lord. God created you whole even before those people and things existed.

Once you understand and accept who God created you to be without hesitation, you'll stop giving individuals handouts on your life. You'll stop putting yourself in compromising positions because you fear that you are lacking stuff, things, and people to make you whole. You are whole with or without stuff, things, and people in your life.

More times than not, God reveals to us how He has made us whole in Him. It's up to you to accept the way He created you and live a life of abundance, knowing that you are whole the way God created you. You have to work on the brokenness within yourself, so that you are truly living the life God ordained you to live.

God took so much time out to create you, and He never makes mistakes. He would never create something that was broken or incomplete. Therefore, remember always that through Him you are made whole.

I am whole, and I am God's masterpiece.

- 1 Thessalonians 5:23 (GNT)
- 1 Peter 5:10 (NIV)
- 2 Corinthians 5:17 (NLT)

Prayer for Today

Lord, please forgive me for all the times that I thought that I was complete because of stuff, things, and people. All I really needed was to realize that the day you thought me into existence, I was already whole through you. Help me to walk each day of my life in the wholeness that you have for me. Heal every single broken piece that is within me. Help me not to place people or things in front of you. Help me reach my potential and anything you add to me will be a bonus for me. Enrich my spirit to have communion with you daily as a reminder that you made me whole. In Jesus' name, amen.

Notes

_____

_____

_____

_____

_____

_____

_____

_____

_____

_____

_____

_____

_____

_____

_____

Day 15: I am a precious creation

Psalm 139:13-14 (ESV)

*For you formed my inward parts;
you knitted me together in my
mother's womb. I praise you, for
I am fearfully and wonderfully
made. Wonderful are your
works; my soul knows it
very well.*

"God created me perfectly in His image. I am a precious creation."

You are so precious to God. He took so much time creating every unique thing about you. We oftentimes don't appreciate what God did when He created us. We oftentimes complain about our bodies, body shaming ourselves. To God, that's a slap in the face. He wants you to love and accept yourself the way you are, with no extras.

Don't you understand that as God's masterpiece, He took His precious time to create you just the way He wanted you?

When we can see ourselves the way God sees us, there is no room to change anything that God already made perfect. Yes! Since you were created in the image of God, you are His precious, perfect creation. Every flaw that you see was created uniquely for you. That should make you feel amazing. That God gave you everything that He wanted you to have and that no one else in this world is exactly like you.

Don't let your negative thoughts, or the thoughts of others, make you feel less than a precious creation from God. When God was creating you, He knew that you would be perfect in His sight. It really doesn't matter how others view you. As long you know that God took precious time to create you and that to Him, you are a precious creation made in His image.

Knowing how much God loves you and how much time He spent on you should make you feel amazing about yourself. The precious gift of life was given to you after God spent His precious time creating you as His masterpiece.

I am a precious creation, and I am God's masterpiece.

- Psalm 119:73-74 (NIV)
- Isaiah 64:8 (NLT)
- Jeremiah 1:4-5 (ESV)
- Ephesians 2:10 (NIV)

Prayer for Today

Lord, I thank you for creating me in your image. I thank you for creating me with your hands and for taking your precious time on me. I no longer want to be envious of others and what they possess; I want to be thankful that you give me everything I need. Remove the thoughts of wanting to alter anything on my body, knowing that you created me uniquely just the way you wanted me to be. Help me to accept myself the way that you created me. Help me to love my flaws because you created them just for me. Help me to love everything about myself the way you love me. In Jesus' name, amen.

Notes

_____

_____

_____

_____

_____

_____

_____

_____

_____

_____

_____

_____

_____

_____

_____

Day 16: I am more than enough

2 Corinthians 9:8 (ESV)

And God is able to make all grace abound to you, so that having all sufficiency in all things at all times, you may abound in every good work.

"I don't have to worry about what I'm not; to God, I am more than enough."

When God created you, He didn't forget to add anything to you; He created you perfect in His sight. The same way that God knows that you are more than enough is the same way He wants you to think of yourself—you lack nothing. Everything that God wanted you to possess in this world is already inside you. You have to know how God feels about you and feel that same way about yourself.

Say to yourself, "I AM MORE THAN ENOUGH."

It doesn't matter who told you that you're a failure, or you'll never be anything in life, or you're not good enough, or you'll never be great. Those individuals didn't create you. Those individuals didn't plant greatness within you. Those individuals don't realize your full potential. Only you have to realize how great an asset you are to this world and start living it.

We often get so down on ourselves, because we think that we are supposed to be like other people, look like other people, and dress like other people. Your uniqueness makes you more than enough. You don't have to copy what you see on television, what you hear on the radio, or what you see on social media. God created you just the way He wanted you to be; you're more than enough.

Starting today, combat every negative thought with a positive one. You're nothing; I'm more than enough. You won't ever be anything in life; I am who God says I am. You need to look like them; God created me fearfully and wonderfully. You won't ever amount to anything; I am more than enough.

I am more than enough, and I am God's masterpiece.

- Philippians 4:13 (NLT)
- 2 Corinthians 12:9 (ESV)
- James 1:4 (NIV)

Prayer for Today

Lord, thank you for creating me more than enough. Help me to not give into the thoughts that come from the enemy that tell me that I am anything less than what you created me to be. I know who I am in you because you told me that I am more than enough. Help me live each day of my life realizing that you created me in your image, and wonderful are your works. Help me to be thankful for the way you intricately wove me together in my mother's womb. I know you didn't make a mistake on me. In Jesus' name, amen.

Notes

_____

_____

_____

_____

_____

_____

_____

_____

_____

_____

_____

_____

_____

_____

I Am God's Masterpiece

Day 17: I am the head and not the tail

Deuteronomy 28:13 (ESV)

And the Lord will make you the head and not the tail, and you shall only go up and not down, if you obey the commandments of the Lord your God, which I command you today, being careful to do them.

"I've realized that it's only up from here."

When God created you, He didn't create you to be in the back; He has called you to be frontline. You have to understand your significance in this world. You were never designed to be at the back or the bottom of anything. You may have started at the bottom, but you won't stay there long. You may have started at the back, but God is slowly moving you into the position that He has created for you.

We must thank God in advance for the position we are in, the position we used to be in, and the position we are headed into. When you obey the commands of God, there is nowhere to go but up. We have to be willing and obedient, not afraid of the position that God wants us to be in. When God positions us as the head, don't forget that you still have an assignment to do. Your position as head doesn't come without a price. God knows that you can accomplish everything He set out for you to do, or He wouldn't have given you the task.

Are you ready to step into the position that God has for you as the head and not the tail?

Get ready for what God is about to do in your life. It calls for you to be frontline. It calls for you to be a leader. It calls for you to be the head and not the tail. It calls for you to be above and not beneath. It calls for you to be in the front and not the back. The calling on your life is greatness; never let anyone tell you otherwise.

I am the head and not the tail, and I am God's masterpiece.

- Deuteronomy 28:1 (NIV)
- Ephesians 2:10 (NLT)
- 2 Corinthians 2:14 (ESV)

Prayer for Today

Lord, thank you for creating me to be the head and not the tail. Help me to never forget whom you created me to be and that I am destined for greatness in this world. Help me to not be cocky or arrogant when you place me in the position that you want me to be in as the head of whatever you have called me to. Prepare me for the ministerial assignments that you have for my life. Build me up to be everything that you need me to be in this world. I thank you for setting me apart and for creating me for greatness. In Jesus' name, amen.

Notes

_____

_____

_____

_____

_____

_____

_____

_____

_____

_____

_____

_____

_____

_____

_____

_____

Day 18: I am a conqueror

Romans 8:37-39 (ESV)

No, in all these things we are more than conquerors through him who loved us. For I am sure that neither death nor life, nor angels nor rulers, nor things present nor things to come, nor powers, nor height nor depth, nor anything else in all creation, will be able to separate us from the love of God in Christ Jesus our Lord.

"I won't be defeated.
I am more than a conqueror."

There are many things in this life that will come at
you in the spirit, in the flesh, and in your mind to
try to defeat you. It's up to you whether you take
the bait or not. Every time something or someone
comes to attack you, God always gives you a way of
escape. All you have to do is stand your ground.
God will always fight on your behalf. Stop thinking
about giving up; you are more than a conqueror.

Are you living life with the mentality that you can
do all things through Christ who gives you
strength?

You have to fight every single day of your life. You
have to fight against the enemy of your soul in the
spirit realm; let him know that he will not win. You
must fight against the negative thoughts in your
mind that tell you negative things about yourself
and others; those thoughts won't prevail. You must
fight against anyone or anything that feeds lies to
you and that goes against God's promises for your
life. God's Word will prevail!

God created you to conqueror everything that will
be placed in your life as a hurdle. God created you
to conquer every storm that will pass through. God
created you to conquer every sickness and disease
that the doctor diagnosed. God created you to

conquer every negative thought that comes raging in your mind. God created you to conquer every fear that you have. You are a conqueror; you have to believe it and walk in it.

I am a conqueror, and I am God's masterpiece.

- 1 John 5:4 (GNT)
- 1 John 4:4 (NIV)
- 2 Corinthians 4:8-10 (ESV)

Prayer for Today

Lord, I know that you created me to be a conqueror in this world. Thank you for not allowing the darts from the enemy to penetrate my spirit or soul. Help me to view life from your perspective, knowing that you have aligned my life with your will. Protect me Lord from things that come to kill, steal, and destroy me. Against those things I know that I am more than a conqueror. Help me to realize that you will not place anything in my way that can't be conquered. Lord, you have created me to conquer everything that comes my way, and for that, I thank you. In Jesus' name, amen.

Notes

_____

_____

_____

_____

_____

_____

_____

_____

_____

_____

_____

_____

_____

_____

I Am God's Masterpiece

Day 19: I am a King's kid

1 John 3:1 (NIV)

See what great love the Father has lavished on us, that we should be called children of God! And that is what we are! The reason the world does not know us is that it did not know him.

"I am heir to the throne.
I am a King's kid."

You have to live every day of your life knowing who you are. You are a King's kid. God is the King of Kings and Lord of Lords and you are heir to His throne. This makes you unique and special in your own right. You are attached to greatness, so only greatness should come from you. You have royalty in your blood, because you come from a royal priesthood. You have to walk all the days of your life knowing that your lifeline is of royal descent.

God has something special for you in this life as heir to His throne. You have to ask Him what He has planned for you and walk in that. You can't be afraid to live out all that God has for you; remember, you are a King's kid. You have privileges that those who aren't royalty possess. You have been set apart; you have been chosen and anointed to live this life that God created you for.

Are you ready to start living your best life as a King's kid?

It's time to take the limits off yourself and off God, so that you can begin to live the best life that God has for you. Greatness literally awaits you! The calling on your life has nothing to do with what you think you deserve in this life, but it has everything to do with what God wants to give you in this life as

His child. Never forget that you didn't create yourself, so you can't possibly know what is best for you. As a child of God (a King's kid) God will allow you to reap the benefits of royalty.

I am a King's kid, and I am God's masterpiece.

- Romans 8:16-17 (NLT)
- John 1:12-13 (ESV)
- Psalm 127:3 (NIV)
- 2 Corinthians 6:18 (NLT)

Prayer for Today

Lord, thank you for creating me heir to your throne. Help me to believe that you made no mistake when you created me. Help me to feel like royalty all the days of my life, as I am a part of your royal priesthood. Anoint me and help me see things from your perspective, as you've already planned out my life. I want to be all that you've called and chosen me to be as a King's kid. I know that greatness awaits me. Help me to walk in the calling that is over my life and the purpose that you've set out for me to accomplish. I thank you for creating me as one of your chosen people. In Jesus' name, amen.

Notes

_____

_____

_____

_____

_____

_____

_____

_____

_____

_____

_____

_____

_____

_____

I Am God's Masterpiece

Day 20: I am walking in purpose

Romans 8:28 (ESV)

And we know that for those who love God all things work together for good, for those who are called according to his purpose.

"I will fulfill the purpose that God has for me."

It's time to walk in your purpose! Before you were born, God knew exactly why He created you. You were not born just by happenstance; you have a purpose here on earth. It's essential to know why God created you to live the life He chose for you. The answer can only come from God Himself. God has a plan for your life already laid out for you, but it's up to you to fulfill the purpose God already predestined for you.

What God has in store for you is nothing short of miraculous. When you walk in your God-given purpose, miracles happen. You didn't create yourself, therefore, you can't tell yourself what you are supposed to do in this world without consulting the Master behind the plan. God has all the answers to your questions about what your purpose is and how you are supposed to fulfill it here on earth.

Are you ready, willing, and able to begin walking in your God-given purpose from this day forward?

Everyone has a purpose, whether they choose to walk in it or not. There is a calling and a special anointing over your life in order for you to fulfill what God has for you. The things that you have to face in this life are building you up in order for you to effectively walk in your purpose. That's why it's important not to try to be in the position of God. You don't know all that you should be doing in this life, but God knows exactly what He designed you to do here on earth.

Don't be scared of the calling on your life. There is only one you! If you don't walk in the purpose God has for you, who will?

I am walking in my purpose, and I am God's masterpiece.

- Psalm 138:8 (NLT)
- Ephesians 1:11 (ESV)

Prayer for Today

Lord, thank you for choosing me for this life. Thank you for the purpose that you have predestined for my life. I know that everything you have for me in this life involves me adhering to your voice and being obedient to your Word. Help me to not be afraid of the calling on my life, but to walk boldly in the purpose you have predestined for me. I'm not worthy of the calling on my life, but thank you for qualifying me by your standards and not the world's standards. Lead me to the individuals who I am supposed to reach and help me to effectively do what you have called me to do here on earth. In Jesus' name, amen.

Notes

_____

_____

_____

_____

_____

_____

_____

_____

_____

_____

_____

_____

_____

_____

_____

_____

I Am God's Masterpiece

Day 21: I am not a failure

1 John 1:9 (NIV)

If we confess our sins, he is faithful and just and will forgive us our sins and purify us from all unrighteousness.

"God's power is made perfect through my weakness."

When God created you, the word failure was not in your DNA. You are not a failure, nor have you ever been, nor will you ever be. Sometimes you don't get things right the first time, so that you can see God's perfect power working through your weakness. Where you are weak, God is strong.

We oftentimes feel like if we don't amount to what others are doing or being in this world, that we are failing at life. That's just not so! God didn't create you a failure. Stop labeling yourself as a failure, because that's not who you are. Don't allow others to label you a failure, because that's not the calling on your life. You've been called to be great in this world. You can't be walking in greatness and be a failure at the same time; you have to choose, and failure should never be the option.

When you frame your mind to think positively, what comes out of your mouth will be positive. Once you realize your full potential, you'll realize that you can do all things through Christ Jesus who gives you strength. You are not a failure. God didn't create you in His image to be a failure in this world. You may not get everything right the first time, but don't let that stop you from trying until you get it right. Don't give up on yourself, because God will never give up on you.

An amazing thing about God is that He placed a calling and an anointing on your life; you just must seek Him and pursue it. From this, you'll realize your full potential and that failure was never intended to be an option for you. Don't ever let Satan trick you into thinking you are a failure.

I am not a failure, because I am God's masterpiece.

- Philippians 1:6 (ESV)
- 2 Corinthians 12:9 (NLT)
- Romans 8:1 (ESV)

Prayer for Today

Lord, thank you for creating each one of us with full potential, a special anointing, and a calling on our lives. Help us to walk in boldness all the days of our lives, knowing that you have called us to greatness. We know that your power is made perfect in our weakness. Thank you for allowing us to be conquerors and not failures in this world. Even if we don't get things right the first time, give us the strength to keep going. Thank you for showing us favor and letting us know how much you think of us because we are made in your image. Continue to push us in the right direction and help us reach our full potential. In Jesus' name, amen.

Notes

_____

_____

_____

_____

_____

_____

_____

_____

_____

_____

_____

_____

_____

_____

_____

_____

I Am God's Masterpiece

Day 22: I am a virtuous woman

Proverbs 14:1 (NIV)

The wise woman builds her house, but with her own hands the foolish one tears hers down.

"I am everything God has called me to be; I am a virtuous woman."

When you think of yourself, think of what God has created you to be in this world. Not by human standards, but by His standards. Not based on what you see on television, what you see on social media, or what anyone has ever told you a woman should be. A virtuous woman has a special calling on her life. She is who God has called her to be instead of whom the world wants her to be.

Do you consider yourself to be a virtuous woman?

It's time to see yourself the way that God sees you. He doesn't view you as the world views you. In fact, if you learn to take on God's perspective in life, you'll see life as you know it differently. Virtue goes beyond charm and beauty. A virtuous woman fears the Lord and is to be praised.

When God created you, He didn't desire for you to compare yourself to anyone else. His desire is that you do exactly what you've been called to do on this earth, because there is no one who can do it like you. So, embrace the fact that you've been called and chosen to be a virtuous woman; it's up to you to walk in the calling or abandon it.

When you say yes to the calling that God has placed on your life, you'll see your life run so much smoother. Not because everything in life is going right, but because your obedience is what God is looking for from you. Never doubt your place in this world and all you've been called to be and do. Walk like you know God chose you and you accept the calling.

I am a virtuous woman, and I am God's masterpiece.

- Romans 12:2 (GNT)
- Proverbs 8:11 (ESV)

Prayer for Today

Lord, thank you for creating me uniquely. I know that you have a special calling and anointing over my life. I want to live up to the standards of being a virtuous woman in this life; help me to live up to my full potential. Don't let me look to the right or to the left of me, but to focus on you and all that you have called me to be. I will always thank you and praise you just for who are. Thank you for creating me for this life. Help me to step into my purpose and fulfill the destiny you have for me. In Jesus' name, amen.

Notes

_____

_____

_____

_____

_____

_____

_____

_____

_____

_____

_____

_____

_____

_____

_____

Day 23: I am handcrafted by God

Ephesians 2:10 (ESV)

For we are God's handiwork, created in Christ Jesus to do good works, which God prepared in advance for us to do.

"God took His precious time when creating me."

You are so precious to God. He didn't just throw you together and say He's satisfied. He took His precious time to intricately knit you together in your mother's womb. You were not created by mere happenstance; no, God knew exactly who He wanted you to be in this world.

When you try to change things about yourself that God intricately put together while you were in your mother's womb, it's a slap in His face. Don't you realize how much of a masterpiece you are because the Master's hands created you? Don't let society tell you that you are too tall or too short, too thin or too big, too light or too dark. Society didn't create you, nor does it know the calling on your life. Don't give into what the world has to offer. God already created you the way He wanted you to be.

After God was done creating you, He looked at you and said, "It's good." You are perfect in God's sight. Nothing that He has ever created has been a mistake. Stop thinking that you should be any other way than what God handcrafted you to be.

Many people get work done on themselves to try to please other people, instead of realizing that the only person you really need to impress is the one who created you. God knows the ins and outs of your life; stop trying to be someone other than who God handcrafted you to be in this world. Take the mask off. Reveal who you truly are to the world with no limitations.

God is not ashamed of who He handcrafted you to be. Are you?

I am handcrafted by God, and I am God's masterpiece.

- Jeremiah 1:5 (NLT)
- Genesis 1:27 (NIV)

Prayer for Today

Thank you, Lord, for creating me to be your masterpiece. Because I was made in your image, I know that you created me just the way you wanted me to be. Help me to accept myself the way you handcrafted me. I don't want to change myself, because then I would no longer be your masterpiece. Help me to walk in boldness and accept all my flaws because you see them as perfectly imperfect. Thank you for taking your precious time on me. In Jesus' name, amen.

Notes

_____

_____

_____

_____

_____

_____

_____

_____

_____

_____

_____

_____

_____

_____

_____

_____

Day 24: I am made perfect in weakness

2 Corinthians 12:9 (NIV)

But he said to me, "My grace is sufficient for you, for my power is made perfect in weakness." Therefore I will boast all the more gladly about my weaknesses, so that Christ's power may rest on me.

"I am made perfect in my weakness."

You are made perfect in your weakness. Where you are weak, it gives God moments to shine on your behalf. It's perfectly okay to boast in your weakness like you would in your strength. In fact, it's better to boast when you are weak and not strong because that shows that God's strength is working through you instead of you working things out in your own strength.

Allow God to work on you and through you with your weaknesses. Stop being afraid to share the areas in your life that you are or once were weak in. God is so amazing that He can turn your weakness into strength without anyone's approval, including your own. You no longer need to be ashamed of the weaknesses you may have. God's strength is made perfect through your weakness.

Are you willing to share your weaknesses so that God's strength is revealed?

Don't ever allow anyone to shame you for the areas you are weak in. With God, anything can change at any time. God can take your weakness today and turn it into your strength for tomorrow. Never underestimate what God can do for you and on your behalf.

Welcome help from God as He shapes and molds you daily. Begin to adhere to His voice daily so that He can groom you into who He wants you to be in this world. Never forget that people who are watching you will get to see your weaknesses turn into strengths, and they will recognize that God was the one in charge of your transformation.

I am made perfect in my weakness, and I am God's masterpiece.

- 1 Corinthians 10:13 (ESV)
- 2 Corinthians 12:10 (NLT)
- 2 Corinthians 13:4 (GNT)

Prayer for Today

Lord, thank you for creating the areas that I am weak in so that your glory can be made manifest in your strength. Help me not be ashamed of my weaknesses, because I know you will soon turn them into strengths. Please keep the devil out of my thoughts and keep my mind stayed on your promises for my life. I am ready for you to turn my weaknesses into strengths, so I surrender every area of my life to you even now. In Jesus' name, amen.

Notes

_____

_____

_____

_____

_____

_____

_____

_____

_____

_____

_____

_____

_____

_____

I Am God's Masterpiece

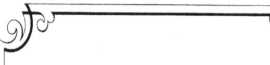

Day 25: I am strengthened

Philippians 4:13 (ESV)

I can do all things through him who strengthens me.

"There is nothing I can't do with God's strength."

Tap into the source from which your strength comes. You aren't strong in your own right, but when God is involved, you are strengthened. There is nothing you can't do in this life. God is the one who gives you the strength to be who He called you to be on this earth. No matter the storms or trials, God gives you the strength to endure.

During those times when you feel lost, lean on God for strength. During those times you feel discouraged, ask God to give you a double portion of His strength. During those times when you lack understanding, ask God to strengthen your discernment. During those times that you feel weak, you are being made perfect through the strength of God.

God is steadily strengthening you for the journey that He has laid out for you. You may not see it now, but everything that He has planned for you requires you to be strengthened by Him in order to succeed. That's why you have to learn to get through the hard times, learn the lessons being taught, and come out even stronger than before.

Find strength in knowing that what God has in store for you is nothing short of amazing. Allow God to be your strength even now for the journey ahead. Remember that the Word of God (the Bible) will strengthen you for the journey, prayer is your best weapon, and praise confuses the enemy.

I am strengthened, and I am God's masterpiece.

- Deuteronomy 31:6 (NLT)
- Isaiah 41:10 (GNT)
- Isaiah 40:31 (NIV)
- Psalm 31:24 (ESV)
- Ephesians 6:10 (NLT)

Prayer for Today

Lord, I know you have equipped me for this life. Thank you for the strength that you have bestowed on me. Continue to strengthen me daily for the journey ahead and help me realize that my strength comes only from you. I'm ready and willing to be used by you for your glory. I know I lack nothing when it comes to you. You've equipped me with everything I need. In any area of my life that I am in lack, strengthen those parts of me. In Jesus' name, amen.

Notes

_____

_____

_____

_____

_____

_____

_____

_____

_____

_____

_____

_____

_____

_____

_____

I Am God's Masterpiece

Day 26: I am predestined for greatness

Ephesians 2:10 (ESV)

For we are his workmanship, created in Christ Jesus for good works, which God prepared beforehand, that we should walk in them.

"Before I entered this world,
God already predestined me for greatness."

God knew who you would be in this world before He placed you in your mother's womb. He predestined you for greatness even before you knew you had a purpose in this world. You've been set up from the beginning of time to do what only you can uniquely contribute to this world. No one in this life is just like you, not even if you're an identical twin. Thank God that He set you apart and predestined you, even before anyone else knew you.

Only God Himself can tell you exactly what He created and predestined you to do here on earth. When you tap into the source from which all things were created, you'll receive all the information that God wants you to acquire for this journey that He has you on. Never underestimate what God is doing for you and through you for His kingdom. Stop looking at what everyone else is doing, focus on what God created you to do, and do just that.

Are you ready for the greatness that God has prepared for you?

Never stop believing that what God has in store for you is anything short of amazing. To receive the greatness that is ahead, you will have to endure all types of trials, tribulations, and tests on the journey, but don't give up. God always prepares us and gives us a glimpse of the end at the beginning. That's why your dreams and goals are so important to God. He has placed greatness within you; you just have to be willing to put in the work to make it come to fruition.

Don't allow anyone to hinder you from reaching your full potential while on this earth. Reach the greatness that God has set out for you daily; you've been destined for greatness since before you were born.

I am destined for greatness, and I am God's masterpiece.

- Jeremiah 29:11 (NLT)
- Romans 8:28-30 (NIV)
- Ephesians 1:11-12 (GNT)

Prayer for Today

Lord, I thank you. Thank you for predestining me for greatness. Show me my purpose and what I am supposed to do in this world according to your will and glory. Remove everything that may be hindering me from reaching my full potential in you. I want to live in my truth and reach the full potential that you have destined for me. Thank you for setting me up for greatness even before you created me in my mother's womb. In Jesus' name, amen.

Notes

_____

_____

_____

_____

_____

_____

_____

_____

_____

_____

_____

_____

_____

_____

_____

_____

I Am God's Masterpiece

Day 27: I am walking in favor

Psalm 90:17 (NIV)

May the favor of the Lord our God rest on us; establish the work of our hands for us— yes, establish the work of our hands.

"I am one of God's favorites;
His favor is all over me."

God gives according to what He wants us to have, so that no one is able to boast about what they have because we didn't obtain them in our own strength. Who you are, what you have, and what you will possess in the future are all from God and the favor that He has bestowed on your life. That's why sometimes we receive blessings, not even knowing where they came from in the physical, but God is always up to something.

Just because you are walking in the favor of the Lord does not mean you should be boasting of all you have, if it's not in reference to being a gift from God and not based on results of your works. You see, we can take the favor of the Lord and act like we had something to do with it. We begin to boast and brag about what we have and how we got it, as if it had anything to do with us resulting from our works. This is the opposite of what God wants you to do. In fact, God wants you to let others know that favor comes from God, so that we can't boast in anyone but Him.

Favor from God shows that He is still in the blessing business. That you are blessed and walking in favor because of the God you serve. That the right people and the right opportunities didn't just start showing up by happenstance, but that they all came through the favor of God. Stop taking credit for what God has done and is still doing in your life.

Do you feel the favor of the Lord all over you? Or have you just been calling it luck all this time?

I am walking in favor, and I am God's masterpiece.

- Psalm 5:12 (ESV)
- Psalm 30:5 (ESV)
- Ephesians 2:8-9 (GNT)

Prayer for Today

Thank you, Lord, for bestowing your favor on my life. I know I don't deserve it and I oftentimes take it for granted. Forgive me for boasting in the things that I know you have accomplished in this life on my behalf. Every time I claimed that I was lucky, I know that blessing came from you and it was you bestowing favor on my life. From here on out, help me to thank you in advance for the favor that is on my life and for being the source from which my help comes. Help me to continue to walk in favor all the days of my life and to always give you the glory that you deserve. In Jesus' name, amen.

Notes

_____

_____

_____

_____

_____

_____

_____

_____

_____

_____

_____

_____

_____

_____

_____

_____

I Am God's Masterpiece

Day 28: I am not a mistake

Philippians 1:6 (ESV)

And I am sure of this, that he who began a good work in you will bring it to completion at the day of Jesus Christ.

"God created me, and
He doesn't make mistakes."

God didn't make a mistake when He created you. In fact, He created you in the image of Himself. Before you were born in this world, God had everything picked out for you. The moment you would be born, what all you would do on this earth, and the moment you will die. All those things should not be taken for granted. Believe that nothing that has ever happened to you or will happen to you has been a mistake. It has all been a part of God's plan for your life.

People may have told you that you shouldn't be this, or you'll never be that. People may have called you ugly, talked about your skin tone, your hair, your clothes, your weight, etc. What you have to do is realize that the way God created you was the way He wanted you to be. Changing things about you is a slap in the face to God. You're basically telling Him that the way He created you was not good enough; think about it.

Don't let what the television, social media, or magazines say that women should look like convince you that the way God created you was a mistake. No one should ever have the power to make you feel less than what God created you to be here on this earth. You are a masterpiece. God created you perfect in His image.

Who or what in this life has made you feel like God made a mistake on you?

It's time to take a stand against anyone who has made you feel less than enough in this world, who has made you feel like God made a mistake on you. You have to declare to yourself today and every day that you are God's masterpiece.

I am not a mistake. I am God's masterpiece.

- Psalm 100:3 (NIV)
- Psalm 138:8 (ESV)
- Romans 8:29(NLT)

Prayer for Today

Thank you, Lord, for letting me know that you created me with purpose and in your image. Thank you for being a God who doesn't make mistakes; therefore, I know you didn't make a mistake on me. Help me to accept myself the way you accept me and to love myself the way you love me. Help me take the power back from those whom I have listened to about the way you created me. I know I am your masterpiece; help me to believe it and walk in it. Thank you for creating me the way that you saw fit. In Jesus' name, amen.

Notes

_____

_____

_____

_____

_____

_____

_____

_____

_____

_____

_____

_____

_____

_____

I Am God's Masterpiece

Day 29: I am blessed beyond measure

Jeremiah 17:7 (NIV)

But blessed is the one who trusts in the Lord, whose confidence is in Him.

"Blessed beyond measure and God is to blame."

Can I tell you a secret? God loves blessing you. That's why even when we don't deserve to be blessed, God continues to bless each one of us. God has always been in the blessing business. He's ready to bless you beyond measure, to give you more than your hands can contain.

Are you ready to be blessed by God?

You have to get in the position where you're ready to receive all that God has for you. This means that you can't be selfish with what you already have. You must be willing to let go of some things in order to receive from God better things. Are you willing to freely give, so that in return, God can freely bestow on you the blessings He has lined up for you?

You see, we are a selfish people. We want all that God wants to bless us with without giving up something in return. When you spend enough time with Jesus, tell Him all about your problems, and He will reveal to you what you need to let go of to receive your blessing. It doesn't necessarily have to be something tangible. It could be to letting go of unforgiveness, letting go of the burdens, letting go of the stress, etc. When you let go, you'll see the blessings begin to flow. Stop holding on to the

I Am God's Masterpiece

things God has told you aren't good for you; it's hindering your blessings from flowing directly to you.

God wants to bless you every single day of your life. Make sure that you aren't doing anything that will hinder those blessings from flowing freely to you.

I am blessed measure, and I am God's masterpiece.

- Deuteronomy 28:6 (NLT)
- Psalm 128:1 (ESV)
- Proverbs 31:28 (NIV)
- 2 Corinthians 9:11 (ESV)

Prayer for Today

Lord, thank you for blessing me much more than I deserve. I know I don't always deserve the blessings you bestow on me, but I appreciate the overflow. Help me give up anything that may be hindering me from receiving the blessings that you have on the way for my life. I don't want to stand in the way of my blessings. As you bless me, Lord, help me to be a blessing to others. I appreciate you and all that you have blessed me with and everything you will bless me with in the future. In Jesus' name, amen.

Notes

_____

_____

_____

_____

_____

_____

_____

_____

_____

_____

_____

_____

_____

_____

_____

Day 30: I'm perfectly made in God's image

Genesis 1:27 (NIV)

So God created mankind in his own image, in the image of God he created them; male and female he created them.

"When God created me, I was perfect in His sight."

When God created you, He looked at you and said, "It's good." You may have flaws, but even your flaws are perfect to God. You were created in the image and likeness of God. He took so much time on you to create you perfectly in His image. When you look at yourself in the mirror, you should see perfection. It's not so that you can be vain about anything, but so you can be thankful that when God was done with you; to Him, you are perfect.

We oftentimes like to critique ourselves or allow others to tear us down based on what they feel we lack. Most of the time, others may not be feeling so great about themselves, so they take it out on you, because you may have what they feel they lack. Don't start picking away at yourself or begin to feel you are in lack in any area. What God has given you was meant for you. How God created you was meant for you. You lack nothing, my dear.

When you look in the mirror, do you see God's perfect creation?

For some women, it's hard to look in the mirror and admit that they are beautiful, gorgeous, or a masterpiece. Why? Because society tells us that we should look a certain way, and if we don't live up to that, then we need to fix something about ourselves. Well, I have news for society. Our creator made us perfect in His image; this means we're masterpieces. This means that we are perfect. This means no mistake was made on me. This means that when I look in the mirror, I should see perfection, no matter what others have said.

Even if you must look yourself in the mirror every day to remind yourself that you are prefect in the image of God, do that. You are a masterpiece, and because God created you, you lack nothing.

I am perfectly made in God's image, and I am God's masterpiece.

- Matthew 19:4 (NLT)
- Mark 10:6 (ESV)
- Ephesians 4:24 (NLT)

Prayer for Today

Thank you, Lord, for creating me in your image. I know I lack nothing since the Master's hands created me. Help me to see the perfection that is me and not to be vain or arrogant about it. I want to be able to look myself in the mirror daily and love who I see, because you created me the way you wanted me to be. Help me to be aware and conscious of those who may shame me, but not to give into what they say. I know I am perfect in your sight and that's all that matters to me. In Jesus' name, amen.

Notes

Day 31: I am God's masterpiece

Ephesians 1:4 (ESV)

Even as he chose us in him before the foundation of the world, that we should be holy and blameless before him.

"I know who I am.
I am God's masterpiece."

When you know who are, you won't allow others to tell you who aren't. We give so much power to others, sometimes unconsciously, but most times consciously. We allow others to sway us in who we are, what we stand for, and even who we are called to be in this world.

You have to be so in tune with who God created you to be in this world that your walk and your talk reflect what God's Word says. Knowing you are God's masterpiece will help you walk like you are God's masterpiece, talk like you are God's masterpiece, and live like you are God's masterpiece.

Have you been living this life like you are God's masterpiece?

God has called you, chosen you, and anointed you for this life. You are made in His image and likeness. So, from today forward, stop acting like you're in lack, because you aren't. Everything God created you to be and do in this world, you can be and do in this world. You lack absolutely nothing.

Reflect daily on what God has said about you so that you don't forget how important you are to Him. If you don't feel like you are important to anyone else in this world, you are extremely important to God. Know that He has a purpose for your life.

I know who I am. I am God's masterpiece.

- Colossians 3:10 (ESV)
- Ephesians 4:24 (NLT)

Prayer for Today

Lord, I thank you for creating me as your masterpiece. Sometimes I feel like I lack in certain areas of my life, but now I know that is not so. Help me to reflect daily on your promises so that I am constantly aware of your presence. Reassure me, Lord, that you have created me for a purpose and that everything will work out for your good. Help me to not only see myself as your masterpiece, but to see others as your masterpiece as well, knowing that you didn't make a mistake on any one of us. In Jesus' name, amen.

Notes

_____

_____

_____

_____

_____

_____

_____

_____

_____

_____

_____

_____

_____

_____

_____

About the Author

Bridgette Marie was raised in Carson, California. She attended Long Beach State where she received her bachelor of arts degree in journalism in 2010. Since she was a young girl, her passion has always been writing. But it wasn't until she was 23 years old that she said yes to the calling that God placed on her life. That calling included pouring empowerment into women and girls of all ages. Bridgette Marie knew that once she shared her testimony, she was sure to win souls for the kingdom of God.

In April 2016, Bridgette Marie published her first book, *In God's Presence, a Daily Devotional,* which has reached far and wide around the globe. Her goal is to encourage, inspire, and uplift others daily, as she strives to reach millions through the gift of writing.

Bridgette Marie is the vice president of Women Blessing Women, a nonprofit organization, and is a dedicated facilitator for the nonprofit Marching Beauties Foundation. These two organizations reach women and girls of all ages, showing them that they are more alike than different.

The promotion of women empowerment is near and dear to the heart of Bridgette Marie. This book was written so that women and girls around the world could affirm themselves and others. If you know who you are, you won't settle for less than who God created you to be in this world.

Made in United States
North Haven, CT
26 December 2022

30151690R00075